TABLE OF CONTENTS

Key West
Conch Cooking

by Joyce LaFray

International Standard Book Number: 0-942084-62-4
Library of Congress Card Catalog Number: 87-51519

For additional copies, write directly to:

Seaside
Publishing, Inc.
P.O. Box 14441
St. Petersburg, Florida 33733-4441

Special thanks to those who have contributed recipes to this collection.

A member of the Publishers Association of the South

Visit our Website: famousflorida.com

She calls the blue-green tropical waters of the Caribbean and the western North Atlantic her home. Staying close to the coast, often near the coral reefs along the bottom of the sea, the great Queen conch gently crawls along.

CONCH: THE EARLY YEARS

During mating season — from early Spring until Fall — the Queen conch (Strombus Gigas) works for hours and even days to lay and bury her eggs in the sand along the sea floor. While she may lay as many as a half million eggs, only a fraction of that number actually live to maturity.

After barely one week, tiny conch hatchlings begin to emerge from the egg cases. Called "veligers," they naturally gravitate toward the surface, swimming around in open waters, drifting wherever the tide and current may take them. In approximately two weeks, they're ready to settle back down into the sand along the bottom of the sea.

Time passes, perhaps even a year, and the little yearlings have begun to develop the distinctive and beautiful shell for which the conch is so famous. By this point, they may be only two to three inches long.

As their development continues, they move along the bottom, feeding on algae, sea grass and other vegetation. Before long — at about three and one-half to four years — the conch develops a broad, flaring outer lip, signifying its sexual maturity.

In her prime, the Queen conch measures about one foot long and weighs up to about five pounds. This is the best time to enjoy her tasty meat. After this point, her growth slows and her flesh tends to become grayish and bitter rather than sweet and white.

A DECORATIVE, USEFUL TREASURE

People have long had a fascination with the beautiful and mysterious Queen conch. Archaeologists have evidence that man has enjoyed her succulent meat as a protein source for hundreds of thousands of years.

While first used for food, the conch also was used extensively for tools, musical instruments and decorative ornaments. The Arawak Indians reportedly used the strong shells to scrape out log canoes. Islanders fashioned hammers, blades, chisels, eating utensils – even cooking pots – from conch shells.

The blowing of a conch horn has been an important form of communication since ancient times. Many used the whole shell as a trumpet, to enhance joyous celebrations, although frequently the conch horn was used to proclaim a death or warn of impending danger.

Soon the conch shell came to be valued as a source for decorative items, as well. Islanders carved lovely pieces of jewelry (necklaces, bracelets, pendants and the like) from the attractive shell, while later Europeans carved exquisite cameos and other unique decorative treasures.

Today, conch shells are a favorite among tourists, who buy hundreds of thousands every year. Still used as musical instruments, experienced conch blowers can play complex melodies on conch trumpets, including Beethoven's Fifth Symphony. Conch blowing contests are held annually in Key West.

"CONCH" ARE PEOPLE, TOO

Pronounced "konk," many natives of Key West and the Bahamas take pride in calling themselves "Conchs."

The nickname probably started during the American Revolution era when Tory sympathizers excaped to the Bahamas claiming, "We'd rather eat conch than fight!" The nickname stuck when their descendents eventually migrated to Key West.

A TASTY SOURCE OF PROTEIN

When properly prepared, the conch is one of the most succulent, tastiest seafood delicacies available. It can be enjoyed raw or cooked, and has been acclaimed widely for its protein content, elegance and versatility.

Conch offers a light and flavorful taste which has been compared with clam, squid, whelk and abalone.

If you are looking for that extra special dish to serve your family and friends, try one of the many recipes in this cookbook; you're in for a real treat!

2

REMOVING THE MEAT FROM THE SHELL

If you look for conch in the market, you'll probably find it in the frozen foods section. Fresh conch is much better, but often hard to find in stores outside the tropics.

While a five pound conch may yield only four ounces of meat, it's worth the effort, if you have the patience, to remove the meat from its shell.

First, using a mallet and a srewdriver, make a hole in the shell at about the third spiral down. Then, carefully insert a knife against the center column of the conch, cutting away the white tendon from the shell's central column.

Next, with a pair of pliers, grip the meat firmly near the claw and slowly, but firmly extract it, pulling to the left and around the contour of the shell. If it resists, check to be sure the tendon has been completely cut away from the shell's central column.

Now you're ready to tenderize it and prepare you dish.

TENDERIZING THE QUEEN CONCH

Once the conch is out of its shell, trim away all appendages and tissue so that you're left with a solid piece of conch meat.

Pound with a heavy metal meat hammer or mallet. If you plan to slice the meat, do so before pounding. Pound to about one and one-half or two times its original size.

To prepare the conch meat for appetizers, chowders and conch burgers, grind with a meat grinder or food processor. For salads, pound and mince, and for stews, pound and then boil or steam for approximately 30 to 45 minutes.

PREPARING CONCH DELICACIES

Now you're ready to try your hand at preparing some of the tastiest dishes you'll ever experience. Since cooking methods vary from island to island and family to family, you'll find this cookbook offers an interesting variety of different recipes from which to choose.

I am delighted to offer these very special recipes to you.

Joyce LaFray

APPETIZERS

HALF SHELL'S CONCH FRITTERS

1	pound conch meat, fresh
1/2	large green or red pepper, diced
1/2	medium onion, diced
1	pickled jalapeno pepper, finely chopped (or any other hot pepper)
1/2 of a	1 - pound box of Aunt Jemima's Pancake Mix
	Peanut oil (or vegetable oil) for frying

Coarsely grind tenderized conch with a meat grinder or food processor and place into a mixing bowl. Be careful to keep the juice. Place green pepper and onion in a sieve and blanch 1 minute in boiling water. To the conch add green pepper, onion, jalapeno, and pancake mix. Mix thoroughly, adding water if necessary. Allow to sit for 30 minutes. With a small scoop or hands, roll balls and make about 1 inch in diameter.

Heat oil to 350° F. Deep fry fritters, a few at a time, until deep golden in color. Serve with cocktail sauce or chili sauce.

Serves: 8-10

From the HALF SHELL RAW BAR, Key West

MANGROVE MAMA'S CONCH FRITTERS

1/2	pound conch, pounded
1	large onion
1	sweet red pepper
1/3	teaspoon salt
1/3	teaspoon black pepper
1/2	teaspoon garlic, chopped
1	teaspoon baking powder
1/3-1/2	cup white flour
1	egg, slightly mixed
	Oil to deep fat fry

Coarsely grind conch in food processor or meat grinder and place into a separate mixing bowl. In a separate bowl, add salt, pepper, garlic powder, and baking powder to flour and stir to mix. Add conch, onion, and red pepper to dry mixture. Add egg and mix well. You may have to add more flour to bind the ingredients. Form mixture into 16 fritters.

Heat oil to 350°F. and fry fritters, a few at a time, until golden. Drain and serve with cocktail sauce, fresh horseradish, or lemon juice.

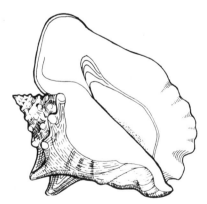

Yield: 12-16

From MANGROVE MAMA'S, Sugar Loaf Key.

VILANO'S CONCH FRITTERS

2	cups conch, tenderized and finely chopped
1	large onion, diced
2	cups self-rising flour
1	green pepper, diced
	Salt and pepper
2	dashes Tabasco sauce
2	eggs, lightly beaten
3/4	cup milk
	Hot Sauce (recipe to follow)

Combine all of the above ingredients with enough milk for the mixture to hold its shape. Form into fritters and fry in 350^0 F. oil until golden. Drain on paper towels and serve with hot sauce, or the sauce of your choice.

HOT SAUCE

3	cups catsup
1/4	cup Worcestershire sauce
3	datil* (or very hot) peppers, finely chopped

Combine all of the ingredients. Makes 1 quart and will keep in a covered glass jar for a week or two.

*Datil pepper can be purchased in the Jacksonville — St. Augustine area of Florida and will be difficult to find elsewhere. Simply substitute any hot peppers.

Serves: 4-6

From the VILANO SEA SHACK, St. Augustine.

CAPTAIN BOB'S CONCH FRITTERS

1	pound conch meat, finely ground
3	cups water
1	teaspoon Accent
1/2	teaspoon garlic powder
1	teaspoon salt
1/2	teaspoon black pepper
3/4	teaspoon oregano
4-6	cups self-rising flour
1/2	cup green pepper, diced
	Oil for frying

Mix water together with Accent, garlic powder, salt, pepper and oregano. Add water slowly to flour until mixture is of drop consistency. Add conch and remaining ingredients. Batter should be stiff enough to drop by teaspoon into oil heated to 350^0 F. Cook until brown.

Yield: 8-10 dozen

From CAPTAIN BOB'S SHRIMP DOCK, Key West

SIPLE'S MARINATED CONCH

(Make 30 days before serving)

5	pounds conch
1	gallon water
1/2	cup salt
2 1/2	cups cider vinegar
3/4	cup olive oil
12	cloves garlic, peeled
	Feta cheese
	Greek olives
	Salonika peppers

First pound conch. This is the secret to making it edible. Use the pointed side of a meat hammer. Pound unmercifully until the muscle portion is riddled with holes. Give special attention to the thicker portion of the muscle.

After your arm recovers from the pounding, boil a gallon of water. Add salt and conch. Cover and lower heat to maintain a steady boil. Allow to cook for 40 minutes, moving conch around occasionally. Remove and cool. Place the cooked conch into sterilized glass jars.

Add vinegar and olive oil to the water and pour to fill jars. Add garlic cloves to jars. Cover tightly. Shake well to mix. Set in refrigerator for at least 30 days. Shake at least one time a week. It will be ready in 30 days, no less.

Cut in julienne strips when ready. Serve with the feta, olives and peppers.

Serves: 10-12

From SIPLE'S GARDEN SEAT, Clearwater.

PAPPAS' MARINATED CONCH

5	pounds conch
1	quart lemon juice
2	large white onions, chopped
1	bunch celery, chopped
3	tablespoons white pepper
3	tablespoons salt
4	limes, squeezed
1/2	cup vegetable oil

Clean and tenderize the conch (see page 3) and then cut into small pieces. Combine all ingredients in a glass bowl. Cover and chill for at least 4 hours before serving.

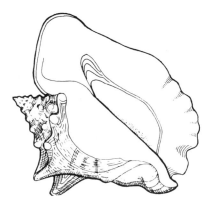

Serves: 10-20

From LOUIS PAPPAS RIVERSIDE RESTAURANT, Tarpon Springs.

PIER HOUSE CARIBBEAN CONCH SEVICHE

(Allow 24 hours for marination time)

1	pound raw conch, finely ground
3/4	cup Key Lime juice or Persian Lime Juice
1	small cucumber, finely chopped
1/2	small red onion, finely chopped
1/2	fresh jalapeno pepper, finely chopped
1/4	red pepper, finely chopped
2	tablespoons chopped parsley
1/3	cup vegetable oil
2 3/4	cup coconut milk
1/2	teaspoon leaf oregano
1	ounce shaved coconut
	Dash Tabasco
1 - 1 1/2	tablespoons sugar
1/2	teaspoon salt
	Dash ground black pepper
	Lettuce
	Bermuda onion, thinly sliced
	Alfalfa sprouts
	Cucumber and fresh basil for garnish

A day ahead: Add finely ground conch to lime juice and marinate for 24 hours. Add cucumbers, onions, peppers and parsley. Drain off excess liquid. After 24 hours, drain off about two-thirds of the lime marinade from the conch mixture. Add pepper mixture, oil, coconut milk, seasonings and vegetables to marinated conch and mix thoroughly.

Serve on a bed of lettuce with thinly sliced bermuda onion, alfalfa sprouts, thinly sliced cucumber and a sprig of fresh basil. Garnish with a fresh Hibiscus flower.

Serves: 6

From THE PIER HOUSE, Key West.

CONCH DIP

1	cup conch, finely ground
1	8-ounce package cream cheese with chives
1	tablespoon milk
1	tablespoon lime juice
1	teaspoon Worcestershire sauce
2	cloves garlic, finely chopped
	Dash of Tabasco sauce
	Black pepper to taste
	Raw vegetables, sliced

Blend the cream cheese and milk together until very smooth.
Add the conch and remaining ingredients.

Serve with fresh raw vegetables.

Yield: 1 1/2 cups

SOUPS &
CHOWDERS

CAP'S BAHAMIAN CONCH CHOWDER

(For a Crowd)

8	pounds diced Bahamian conch (tenderized and cooked in pressure cooker about 30 minutes)
1	pound salt pork, chopped
2	pounds butter or margarine
4	pounds onions, chopped
4	cups flour
4	46-ounce cans clam juice, or
6	quarts fresh clam juice
2	32 - ounce cans tomato juice
2	No. 10 cans Libby crushed tomatoes (6 quarts)
2	stalks celery, peeled and chopped
6	pounds carrots, peeled, chopped and cooked
12	pounds potatoes, diced and cooked
1/2	cup Accent® (optional)
2	tablespoons white pepper
2	tablespoons cayenne
1	fifth dry sherry wine

Melt the butter or margarine in a very large pan and saute the salt pork and onions until golden over medium heat. Stir in the flour and cook until slightly brown. Add the clam juices and tomato juice, a little at a time, stirring constantly. Add the conch and the rest of the ingredients and mix. Simmer until the vegetables are tender.

Serves: 40-50

From CAP'S SEAFOOD RESTAURANT, St. Augustine

CREAMY CHILLED CONCH CHOWDER

(Allow 5 days to marinade conch)

2	cups fresh conch, finely ground (about 1 pound)
2	cups Old Sour (see page 35)
4	medium cucumbers, seeded, diced but not peeled
1	clove garlic, finely minced
1	dash Tabasco sauce
1/4	teaspoon celery seed
1/8	teaspoon ground bay leaves
1/2	teaspoon dill weed
1/4	teaspoon rosemary
1/4	teaspoon white pepper
3	cups plain yogurt
1	cup sour cream
	Parsley for garnish

Place the conch meat in a bowl. Add Old Sour until conch meat is just about covered. Cover bowl and refrigerate for 5 days and the juices will marinate the meat. Stir about twice each day, and add more Old Sour if required. After 5 days drain and discard marinade.

Place cucumbers and garlic in a sauce pan and cover with water. Simmer just until the cukes look glassy. Drain. Add the Tabasco sauce, celery seed, bay leaves, dill weed, rosemary and pepper. Chill. When cucumber mixture is cold, add the yogurt, sour cream and the marinated (and _drained_) conch meat. Refrigerate until ready to serve and then sprinkle each serving with parsley.

Serve in coffee cups with Cuban bread slices fried in garlic butter on the side, or in small cups garnished with herb flavored croutons, grated raw carrots, chopped scallions, alfalfa, sieved hard boiled eggs, thinly sliced green bell pepper or radishes. This chowder keeps for at least a week tightly covered in the refrigerator.

Yield: 2 quarts

EASY CONCH CHOWDER

2 1/2	cups finely minced conch
1/2	pound butter or margarine
2	onions, finely chopped
3	stalks celery, finely minced
1	carrot, finely minced
1	bird pepper* or other hot pepper, chopped
2	quarts fish stock**
2	large potatoes, finely minced
	Salt, pepper and fresh thyme to taste
1	quart heavy cream

Saute onions, celery and carrot in butter until onions are soft but not browned. Add the conch and remaining ingredients except the heavy cream. Simmer until vegetables are fully cooked. Add heavy cream and cook just until heated. Do not boil! Serve immediately.

*These small peppers are found in the Florida Keys. If not available you may substitute any small pepper that is very hot (spicy).

**To prepare, add to 2 cups of water and 1 cup white wine the following: 2 onions, parsley stems, 1 carrot, 1 stalk celery. Simmer 20 minutes and strain.

Serves: 10-12

CAPTAIN BOB'S CONCH CHOWDER

1/3	cup onion, diced
2	tablespoons cooking oil
3	1 - pound cans potatoes, drained and diced
2	teaspoons Kitchen Bouquet
2	teaspoons oregano
1	teaspoon black pepper
2	teaspoons salt
1	bay leaf
2	teaspoons Accent
1/2	teaspoon garlic powder
2 1/2	pounds conch
3-4	stalks celery
1-2	large carrots
1/3	cup tomato paste
1/4	cup green pepper, diced
3-4	quarts water

In large pot saute onion in oil. Add potatoes and seasonings. Grind conch, celery, and carrots until fine. Add to pot along with tomato paste and green pepper. Add 3-4 quarts water. Cook over medium-low heat for 4-5 hours .

Serve or cool if you have extra. (Make sure the soup is cool before refrigeration, otherwise the conch will sour).

Yield: 1 1/2 gallons

From CAPTAIN BOB'S SHRIMP DOCK, Key West.

CAPTAIN JIM'S MINORCAN CONCH CHOWDER

3/4	pound conch meat, well cleaned, pounded, and finely ground
1/8	pound salt pork, chopped fine
2	onions, chopped fine
1	bell pepper, chopped fine
1-2	datil* peppers
3	cups canned tomatoes, chopped
2	cups canned potatoes, diced
1/2	cup tomato puree
1/2	tablespoon thyme
1/2	tablespoon salt
1/2	tablespoon ground pepper
1-2	bay leaves, crushed

Saute salt pork in large pot. Remove and set aside. To the grease add onions and bell peppers and saute. Add hot datil peppers. Add reserved salt pork , conch and remaining ingredients. Bring to boil for about 15 minutes. Simmer 45 minutes to 1 hour.

*Datil peppers are very hot and may be difficult to find. Substitute any very hot pepper.

Serves: 6-8

From CAPTAIN JIM'S CONCH HUT, St. Augustine.

CONCH BEAN SOUP

(Allow 24 hours to prepare ahead)

1	cup conch, tenderized and finely chopped
1	pound lima or navy beans
1	can crushed tomatoes
2	large onions, diced
1/2	bird pepper*
1	ham bone
	Salt and coarsely ground pepper to taste

Soak beans overnight. In the morning drain the beans and add fresh water and cook until half done. Add the tomatoes, onions, pepper and the ham bone, the seasonings and the conch.

*These are very hot peppers found in the Florida Keys. Substitute any very hot pepper.

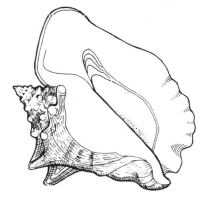

MARINA POLVAY

MARKER 88's CONCH BISQUE

8-12	ounces conch meat; cleaned, peeled and ground*
2	quarts cold water
	Bouquet garni**
2	tablespoons salt
4	tablespoons flour
2	tablespoons butter
1/2	cup heavy cream
	Sherry wine

Place the conch meat, cold water, bouquet garni and salt in large pan and bring to a boil. Simmer 1 1/2 hours. Discard bouquet garni. Strain soup and put meat aside, reserving broth.

In a sauce pan, make a roux*** with butter and flour. Add strained soup, stirring constantly until thickened slightly. Add conch. Return to boil and simmer 15 minutes more. Add cream and heat. Serve with sherry on the side to be added according to taste.

*NOTE: Grind in a meat grinder or food processor.

** **Bouquet Garni**

2	sprigs fresh parsley
1	stalk celery
1	leek
1	large piece fresh ginger halved

Tie all together with string.

***Roux:** Melt butter and stir in flour. Cook stirring constantly for several minutes until golden or brown as recipe indicates.

Serves: 4

From MARKER 88 Restaurant , Plantation Key.

SALADS

KEY WEST CONCH SALAD

(Allow 24 hours for marination time)

1	cucumber, peeled, seeded, finely chopped
1	pound conch
	Juice of six limes
1/2	red onion, finely chopped
1/2	red pepper, finely chopped
1/2	cup cilantro (or Chinese parsley or coriander)
1	cup olive oil
1	level teaspoon leaf oregano
1	level teaspoon sugar
1/2	level teaspoon salt
1/2	level teaspoon ground black pepper

Chop conch into 1/8 inch pieces, cover with lime juice. Marinate for 24 hours. Drain. Add onions, cucumbers, cilantro and bell pepper finely. Combine remaining ingredients. Refrigerate for 24 hours.

Serves: 4

From THE PIER HOUSE, Key West.

PAUL'S CONCH SALAD

(Allow time to marinate overnight)

1	pound conch meat
1/2	bunch scallions (both green and white parts), chopped
1/2	medium onion, chopped
1	medium tomato, chopped
1/2	bell pepper, chopped
1/4	stalk celery, chopped
2/3	cup olive oil
1/2	cup vinegar
2/3	cup lemon juice (about 3 lemons)
	Dash black pepper
	Oregano for garnish

Pound conch meat for 10-15 minutes to tenderize it. Cut into 1/2-inch pieces. Place in glass or pottery bowl. Add chopped vegetables, oil, vinegar, lemon juice, and black pepper. Mix well. Taste for seasoning. Marinate overnight or for at least 8 hours. Serve on a colorful decorated plate. Sprinkle oregano to taste on top.

Serves: 4-6

From PAUL'S RESTAURANT, Tarpon Springs.

PRAWNBROKER CONCH SALAD

(Allow 24 hours for marination time)

2 1/2	pounds conch
1	cup lime juice
1/2	cup white vinegar
1/2	cup vegetable oil
1	tablespoon Worcestershire sauce
2	cups coarsely chopped red onions
5	jalapeno peppers, chopped
2	cups coarsely chopped green peppers
2	cups coarsely chopped celery
2	cups coarsely chopped tomatoes

Chop tenderized conch in container of food processor or by hand. Combine all marinade ingredients. Marinate conch in refrigerator for 24 hours. Drain marinade from chopped conch. Toss conch with salad ingredients. Refrigerate.

Serve chilled on a bed of lettuce.

Serves: 12-16

From the PRAWNBROKER, Ft.Myers.

CONCH SALAD

2	4-6 ounce conchs
1	medium onion
1/2	bell pepper
1/2	cup olive oil
	Juice of three Key limes or 1 Persian lime
1	clove garlic, minced
1	teaspoon parsley
1/2	teaspoon oregano
1	tablespoon vinegar
1	teaspoon salt
1/2	teaspoon curry powder or to taste
	Old Sour to taste (see page 35)
2	avocados

Grind or finely chop the conch, onion, and bell pepper. Place in a bowl; cover with oil, lime juice, vinegar, and other condiments. Mix well and place in refrigerator overnight. When ready to serve, heap into halved avocados and serve very cold, either as an appetizer or as a salad.

Serves: 4

CONCH AND AVOCADO SALAD

(Allow time to marinate overnight)

2	4-6 ounce conchs, ground or pounded and finely minced
1	medium onion, finely chopped
1	green pepper, finely chopped
1/2	cup olive oil
1	Persian lime, or 3 tablespoons lime juice
1	tablespoon vinegar
1	clove garlic, peeled and mashed
1	teaspoon parsley, chopped
1/2	teaspoon thyme
1	teaspoon curry powder
2	avocados, halved and seeded
	Salt, pepper and Old Sour (see page 35) to taste

Marinate overnight the conch, onion and green pepper in the oil with the juice from the lime, vinegar, and spices in a covered bowl. Refrigerate. To serve, spoon the mixture into halved avocados. Add salt, pepper and Old Sour to taste. Serve chilled.

Serves: 4

From the KEY WEST WOMAN'S COOKBOOK, Mrs. Emily Wooley Goddard.

MAIN
COURSES

BAHAMIAN CRACKED CONCH

1	4 - 6 ounce tenderized conch steak
1	cup herbed flour* for dredging
4	eggs
1	cup milk
3	teaspoons clarified butter**
2	tablespoons lime juice (Key limes preferrably)

Tenderize conch steak with a hammer until the conch surface area doubles in size. This will take at least 10 minutes. Dredge steak in herbed flour. Dip in egg wash made by mixing 4 eggs with 1 cup milk. Dredge back in flour while heating butter. Saute conch in clarified butter for 30 seconds over high heat. Turn. Lower heat. Add Key lime juice to butter, mix and serve with butter sauce over the cracked conch.

Herbed flour: Flour with salt, pepper, thyme, and a pinch of baking powder.

**Clarified Butter: Slowly heat butter until completely melted. Carefully skim off the whey (white matter) that rises to the top. The remaining clear butter will keep for at least a week if tightly covered refrigerated.

Serves: 1

From the BAGATELLE, Key West.

CRACKED CONCH

4   4-6 ounce conch
1   egg, beaten
       Flour
       Salt and pepper
       Vegetable oil

Pound conch until tender (about 10 minutes). Flip conch into egg.
Roll on both sides into flour seasoned with salt and pepper. Fry in
oil at low heat until brown on both sides.

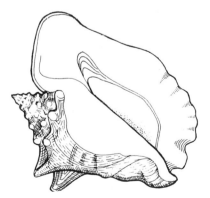

Serves: 2

SAUCED CONCH

3	4-6 ounce conch
2	tablespoons brown sugar
1	onion, chopped
1	clove garlic, chopped
2	tablespoons celery, chopped
1	tablespoon curry powder
1	teaspoon scallions
1	teaspoon thyme
2	tablespoons butter mixed with 1 garlic clove, minced
1	teaspoon cornstarch
2	tablespoons ketchup

"Beat the hell out of the conch with a wooden meat tenderizer.*"
Put the conch in a large pot with enough water to cover, and boil for
45 minutes. Drain and reserve the liquid.

In a saute pan, carefully melt the brown sugar, so as not to burn.
When melted, add the onion, garlic, celery, curry, scallions, thyme,
and garlic butter. Blend well. Add the conch and saute until brown.

Add the cornstarch to 1/2 cup of the liquid left from boiling the
conch. Pour the cornstarch mixture and ketchup into the conch
mixture and mix well to thicken. Simmer for about 6 minutes.

*This is a direct quote from the owner of *Delicious Landings Restaurant*, Terri Lambert.

Serves: 3

From the DELICIOUS LANDINGS RESTAURANT, Grenada, West Indies.

CONCH PARMESAN

4	4-6 ounce conch steaks, well-tenderized*
2	cups herbed tomato sauce **
1	egg
1/2	cup milk
1/2	cup Italian flavored breadcrumbs
3	ounces mozzarella cheese, grated
3	ounces Swiss cheese, grated
3	ounces Parmesan cheese, grated
	Vegetable oil for frying

With a wire whisk beat the egg and milk together well. Dip the tenderized conch into this mixture then into the breadcrumbs. Deep fry until golden brown and drain on paper towels or brown paper bags.

Preheat oven to 350⁰ F. Grease a baking dish. Pour tomato sauce to cover the bottom. Arrange conchs on top of sauce. Pour the remaining sauce over the steaks, reserving about 1/2 cup. Mix together the cheeses and spread over the top layer of sauce. Top with remaining sauce and bake for about 15 minutes or until cheese is melted. Serve two steaks per person.

*Pound at least 10-15 minutes

**Available at most supermarkets, or prepare your own.

Yield: 2 servings

From THE CRACKED CONCH CAFE, Vaca Key,

MANGROVE MAMA'S CONCH STEAK

1	4-6 ounce conch steak,
	Flour
1	egg, beaten
	Clarified butter*
1/2	teaspoon lemon juice
1	tablespoon dry white wine
	Salt to taste

Butterfly conch steak by cutting out the vein, sliding knife down each side, and opening steak out to each side. Tenderize by pounding with mallet or back of a knife. Dredge steak in flour, dip in beaten egg, and back again into flour. Saute over medium heat in clarified butter, about 45 seconds on each side. Add lemon juice, wine, and salt to taste. Serve immediately.

*Clarified Butter: Slowly heat butter until completely melted. Carefully skim off the whey (white matter) that rises to the top. The remaining clear (clarified) butter keeps for at least a week if tightly covered and refrigerated.

Serves: 1

From MANGROVE MAMA'S, Sugar Loaf Key.

CONCHBURGS

2	cups conch, ground
1	medium sized onion, finely minced
1/2	of a hot pepper, finely diced, seeds removed
1	tablespoon olive oil
1	egg, well-beaten
1	teaspoon fresh parsley, finely minced
	Dash of Tabasco or other hot sauce
1	cup fresh breadcrumbs
	Salt and ground pepper to taste
	Kaiser Rolls or hamburger buns
	Sliced onions

Mix together the conch, onion and hot pepper. Add oil, egg, parsley and Tabasco sauce and mix well. Add the bread crumbs or enough breadcrumbs to shape into burger patties. Broil until browned well. Serve with large slices of onion and Old Sour (see page 35). Serve on fresh Kaiser rolls or hamburger buns.

Serves: 6

SAUCES &
CONDIMENTS

OLD SOUR*

1   cup Key Lime juice**
1   tablespoon salt
2   whole bird peppers, a few drops of hot sauce,
         or cayenne to taste

Add the salt and peppers or hot sauce to the juice. Allow to let it stand at room temperature for one or two days. Strain through cheesecloth until liquid is clear. Bottle tightly with cork and store at room temperature in an "out-of-the-way" place for two to four weeks.

*A favorite potent sauce for use on conch and broiled, baked or fried fish. True "conchs" rarely eat seafood without a few drops of the native juice. Bird peppers are peppers native to the Florida Keys, but other "hot" peppers will do.

**May substitute Persian lime juice, sour orange or lemon juice.

Yield: 1 cup

CONCH PESTO MARINARA SAUCE

1	cup finely chopped conch
2	tablespoons olive oil
2	shallots, chopped
4	cloves garlic, chopped
1	pint tomatoes, peeled and diced
1/2	cup tomato puree
1	pint tomato juice
1/2	bunch parsley
1	bunch basil
1/4	cup fresh butter
1	pound cooked pasta or noodles

Saute shallots, add garlic and saute. Add tomato and puree.
Simmer for 1/2 hour, add conch and simmer 1/2 hour more. Add
herbs and butter. Serve over pasta.

Serves: 8

From THE GARDEN TERRACE RESTAURANT, Miami.

re-order information

Copy this form and send to:

$\mathcal{Seaside}$
Publishing, Inc.
P.O. Box 14441
St. Petersburg, Florida 33733-4441

Please send me _____ copies of **Famous Florida!**® Classic Conch **Cooking** at $5.95 per copy. Add $2.50 for postage and handling for the first book ordered and .50 for each additional copy. Make check payable to *Seaside Publishing*

Name _____

Street _____

City _____

State & Zip _____

Meet The Author

Joyce LaFray, acknowledged to be one of Florida's foremost food experts, has earned plaudits for her ability to educate and entertain in a cornucopia of settings. As author, restaurant reviewer, lecturer, publisher and editor, she has developed a rapidly growing, enthusiastic group of fans that trail her food paths in Florida and throughout the world.

Her readers have faithfully followed her exploits and adventures in the fields of food, wine, and travel, via a myriad number of cookbooks and restaurant guides. She has written for many newspapers and magazines, including Creative Loafing, Gourmet Retailer, Where, Florida Epicure, and others.

Some of the honors and awards bestowed on her efforts include a proclamation for a "Joyce LaFray Day" by the Mayor of the City of Miami for her excellence and dedication to food journalism. She has received Certificates of Appreciation from the University of Florida Institute of Food and Agricultural Sciences and "Best of State Award" for her contributions to Adult Education Programs.

Internationally, Joyce has lived in Rome Italy, and has traveled extensively as host of television's "Tropic Cooking" series and radio's popular "Eat It!" in Tampa Bay. She has been an honored guest of many governments including Italy, Spain and the Caribbean islands, Belgium, Greece and Cuba. She has participated in numerous food and wine events throughout the United States, South America and Europe as journalist and judge.

The list of nationally distributed books written by Joyce LaFray includes: Tropic Cooking: The New Cuisine of Florida and the Caribbean (Ten Speed Press), Seafood!" Famous Florida! Restaurants & Recipes, The Underwater Gourmet, The Key Lime Cookbook, Conch Cooking, Crab Cooking, Key Lime Desserts, Florida Orange Recipes, Country Cookin', Cracker Cookin', Guide to Florida's Best Restaurants (Ten Speed Press) and Cuba Cocina: The Tantalizing Flavors of Cuba, Yesterday, Today and Tomorrow (HarperCollins).

8/30/00

re-order information